A VISIT TO
MEXICO

By Mary Packard
Illustrated by Benrei Huang

A GOLDEN BOOK • NEW YORK
Western Publishing Company, Inc., Racine, Wisconsin 53404

Juanito Ramírez lives in Mexico with his mother, father, brother, and four sisters. His father is a silver craftsman in their hometown of Taxco. About seventy miles southwest of Mexico City, Taxco is a lovely small colonial city with cobblestone streets and red-tiled roofs.

The thing Juanito likes best about his house is that it is built around a courtyard with a comfortable patio and cheerful garden. This is his favorite place to play.

Juanito and his oldest sister were born on the same date.

"Only four more days until our birthday, Lupita!" said Juanito on their way to breakfast. "I can't wait until our party!"

"Not *our* party this year, Juanito," Lupita corrected him gently. "Have you forgotten how old I'm going to be—that I will be having a party of my own?"

Juanito counted the years on his fingers. "I'm going to be six, so you are going to be fifteen."

"That's right," said Lupita. "And when a girl turns fifteen, she becomes a *señorita*," she explained. "It will be my *quince años*."

"That's why we're going to have a special party for Lupita," added their mother, Señora Ramírez.

Juanito hoped that when Lupita turned into a *señorita*, she would still have time to spend with him.

The next morning before school, Juanito went to the *mercado* with Lupita. They bought avocados, *chiles*, tomatoes, and a pale green fruit called *chayote*. They also bought a bag of black beans and *tortillas*, which look like very thin pancakes. Everywhere they went, the shopkeepers said, "You are going to be a *Quinceañera*, Lupita."

"I certainly am!" was Lupita's happy reply.

Bending down to whisper in Juanito's ear, Lupita confided, "When I am fifteen, everyone will call me Señorita Ramírez."

"Will I have to call you that, too?" Juanito whispered back.

"Of course not, silly," Lupita said with a laugh, giving him a hug.

On their way home, Juanito stopped to admire the *piñatas* in Don Diego's shop.

"Lupita, look at the star hanging next to the *burrito*. Isn't it wonderful?" he said.

"It certainly is," replied Lupita.

"If I were having a big party this year," said Juanito, "that's the one I'd like to have."

At the midday meal, everyone chatted happily about Lupita's *quince años* ball.

"The dressmaker called to say that your gown is ready," announced Señora Ramírez.

"Don't forget to pick out flowers for your corsage," reminded Rosa, Lupita's sister.

"Has everyone answered the invitations?" asked Señor Ramírez."

"Yes, and they are all coming," replied Lupita with a big smile.

"I wonder if anyone will even remember that it's my birthday, too?" Juanito thought.

That night, as Juanito and his brother, Roberto, were getting ready for bed, they heard music outside their window. Juanito pulled the curtain aside and peeked out.

"Look!" he exclaimed. "It is a *mariachi* band. They're dressed in costumes and singing!"

"That's the *Mariachi Aguila*," said their father, who had just come into the room. "I hired them to sing for Lupita. Now that she's almost grown-up, she will have plenty of *serenatas* to amuse her."

Juanito covered his ears. He had heard enough about Lupita's birthday for one day!

The next day was Juanito's birthday.

As he was leaving for school, he noticed that Lupita and their mother were hanging strings of colored lights around the patio.

"They must be starting to get ready for Lupita's party," he thought.

Juanito's mother came for him after school.

"I have a few errands to do before we go home," she said. "But they won't take long. I promise."

While his mother picked up Lupita's gown from the dressmaker, Juanito looked for a present for his sister. In one of the many silver workshops on the plaza, he found a silver butterfly pin. The silversmith smiled as Juanito counted out the *pesos* he had been saving. Then the silversmith wrapped the pin for Juanito and tied the package with a bright bow.

"Home at last," said Juanito. "Maybe someone sent me a greeting," he added as he peeked into the mailbox.

But there was not even one letter. Sighing heavily, he went into the house.

"Surprise!" came a shout. Then everyone popped out from hiding places. All of Juanito's friends and family were there.

Lupita led them into the garden. Juanito couldn't believe his eyes.

"My *piñata*, the star!" he exclaimed. "But what about your *quince años*?" he asked Lupita.

"That's tomorrow night at the church hall and then—the great ball," she answered. "You didn't think we could fit everyone in here, did you?"

The food was delicious. There were *pozole*, a kind of delicious stew, and *tostadas*, toasted tortillas topped with cream and cheese. Then, a custardlike dessert called *flan*.

"It's time to break the *piñata*," Señor Ramírez called out.

Wearing a blindfold, Juanito and each of his friends took turns batting at the *piñata* with a stick. Finally it broke, showering them all with candy and little toys.

Juanito's father played his guitar as the guests sang "Las Mañanitas," the traditional birthday song, while Juanito was cutting his birthday cake.

"This is my best birthday ever, Lupita," Juanito said with a grin.

<u>Facts About Mexico</u>

• Mexico has thirty-one states and the Federal District, which is more commonly known as Mexico City. It is the capital of Mexico and has a population of more than nineteen million.

• The Aztec Indians were the rulers of much of Mexico for almost two hundred years until the Spanish conquered them. The Aztecs liked chocolate so much that they used cocoa beans for money.

• There are so many volcanoes in Mexico that it is said that no one has ever counted them all.

• The most popular sport in Mexico is *futbol,* or soccer. Most Mexican boys dream of growing up to be a soccer player or a bullfighter. Mexicans also enjoy baseball almost as much as Americans do. A unique spectator sport is called *fronton,* or *jai lai,* which is played with a curious wicker basket/bat. An amateur version, *frontenis,* is played with a tennis racquet and a special ball that is hit against a wall.

• In Mexico, people eat their main meal at midday. In small towns, this is usually followed by a nap called a *siesta.* Stores close for *siesta* and reopen at three o'clock.

• Mexicans enjoy rodeos, called *charriadas,* where horsemen called *charros* display their amazing skills.